Genuine Articles
Teacher's Manual and Answer Key

Genuine Articles

Authentic reading texts for intermediate students of American English

Teacher's Manual and Answer Key

Catherine Walter

CAMBRIDGE
UNIVERSITY PRESS

Published by the Press Syndicate of the University of Cambridge
The Pitt Building, Trumpington Street, Cambridge CB2 1RP
40 West 20th Street, New York, NY 10011-4211, USA
10 Stamford Road, Oakleigh, Melbourne 3166, Australia

First published 1986
Second printing 1993

Printed in the United States of America

Library of Congress Cataloging in Publication Data
Walter, Catherine, 1946 –
Genuine articles.
1. English language – Text-books for foreign
speakers. 2. Readers – United States. 3. English
language – Study and teaching – Foreign speakers.
I. Title.
PE 1128.W343   1986   428.6′4   85-10993

ISBN 0-521-27801-5 teacher's manual : paperback
ISBN 0-521-27800-7 student's book : paperback

Cover design by Frederick Charles Ltd.
Book design by Peter Ducker

Contents

Acknowledgments   vii
Introduction   ix

Part 1   Instructions: How to do things

1 **How to shine at a job interview**   1
2 **How to protect yourself**   2
3 **How to save a life**   5
4 **How to win at marriage**   7

Part 2   Descriptions: What things are like

5 **Athens is dying**   11
6 **Zen and the art of motorcycle maintenance**   13
7 **Vacationing in Mexico**   16
8 **Men of the Pine Barrens**   18

Part 3   Processes: How things happen

9 **Power**   21
10 **Smoke signals**   23
11 **Lions at work and play**   25
12 **Burnout**   27

Part 4   Narrative: What happened

13 **The diamond**   31
14 **A gentleman thief**   33
15 **Great operatic disasters**   36
16 **Poison**   37

Contents

Part 5   *Persuasion: Why you should do it*

17 The family room   40
18 Better left unsaid   42
19 Save the children   43
20 Two letters   46

Part 6   *Categories: How things are classified*

21 Men and women: Some differences   49
22 Getting to the airport   51
23 How personality affects your health   53
24 Wonder wander   55

Acknowledgments

I owe many of the ideas in this book to teachers I have worked with, trained, or observed over the years. I am sorry that my memory is not good enough to acknowledge them all by name.

I should like to thank Viviane Dunn for the *Designing an animal* exercise in Unit 11; Jacqueline Rodrigues for the *Discussion* technique in Units 2, 8, 14, and 18, and Michael Swan (in *Spectrum: Teacher's Book*, Cambridge University Press, 1980) for the *Misleading instructions* exercise in Unit 2.

Introduction

This book is intended for teachers using *Genuine Articles* in the classroom. Some parts of it will also be useful to students working independently at improving their reading skills. The main aims of the Teacher's Manual, however, are
- to give teachers guidance in exploiting the texts and exercises of the Student's Book in the classroom and
- to provide additional activities for speaking, vocabulary, and writing work based on the topics of the texts.

The reading process

Reading can be seen as a process of re-creating the text in the reader's mind. Another way of putting this is to say that the reader matches the elements of the text against his or her own ideas about the world and modifies those ideas accordingly. Research done at Brunel University* with the aid of a machine that records readers' progress through a text has brought powerful support to this idea. Native English-speaking students were presented with a text whose content and vocabulary were difficult for them. Those who read most effectively, as measured by summary writing and by objective tests, were those who defined the structure of the text for themselves as they read – they seemed to build a summary in their minds. In fact, significantly more students did well when they were told that they would have to write a summary of what they read. More of these students had good scores on *both* objective tests and summary writing than students who expected only objective tests after reading.

  Genuine Articles seeks to exploit these findings in helping language learners to read English better. Intermediate students will often find themselves in the same situation as the students in the Brunel experiment: faced with a text that is a little too difficult and that contains several unknown words. The *Summary skills* exercises that follow most of the texts in this book aim to develop in learners the same technique that the successful students in the Brunel experiment used. This consists of a first careful reading with pauses to think, followed by a "read-and-search." In the read-and-search, the successful Brunel readers read the beginning of the text, then skipped to other parts of the text (presumably to look at related points) before resuming where they had left off. They read smoothly again for a while, and then skipped around again, and so on. The *Summary skills* exercises make students follow the same kind of process, searching in the text for related points. This is why the exercises are almost always printed facing the text itself, to encourage successful reading habits. Different

*L. Thomas and S. Augstein, "An experimental approach to the study of reading as a learning skill," *Research in Education 8*, November 1972, pp. 28–45.

approaches to the summary-building process are used throughout the book, in order to accommodate different cognitive styles.

In addition, there are a number of easily defined, discrete skills that have been shown to be powerful tools for understanding a difficult text. Among these, for example, are skill in guessing unknown words from context and the ability to infer information that is implicit in the text. So the *Summary skills* exercises are followed in each case by tasks that develop these mini-skills. One mini-skill is practiced in each exercise, in order to give students a clear idea of what they are learning and to increase motivation.

Authentic texts

The criteria used for the choice of texts in *Genuine Articles* are explained in the teacher's introduction to the Student's Book. Variety of discourse function, variety of subject, and variety of source were the three principles used. In all cases but two the texts are reproduced word for word (although often shortened); the exceptions required slight adaptation to make the shortened text flow better, but no texts were simplified in any way.

One could object that using authentic texts does not necessarily make for authentic reading, since the students are reading for completely different purposes than they would in the "real world." This is true of any collection of language-teaching texts; but some compensation is made by

a) providing a suggestion for a warm-up activity for each unit in the Teacher's Manual. This is designed to get the students thinking about the topic of the text.

b) giving an introduction to each text, to situate it in context. Thus the student is not placed in the position of using the first reading to guess what kind of text it is.

c) replacing the *Summary skills* exercise, in some cases, by an exercise called *Reading for specific information*, which usually directs the students' attention to certain aspects of the text.

d) letting the students choose, in some instances, which aspect of a text they want to concentrate on. For an example, see the *Summary skills* exercise of "Save the children" on page 69 of the Student's Book.

Using the Student's Book in the classroom

The order of the units in the Student's Book is determined by the functional categories into which the texts fall. Thus, each group of four units contains texts with the same function or purpose (for example, categorization or instructions). But the units do not have to be done in order. Teachers who have organized their programs around a series of themes can use the texts in the order in which they relate to those themes. Complete instructions are given for each exercise, even if one of the same type has appeared in a previous unit.

It is inevitable that some texts will appeal to you more than others. But it might be worth considering that texts that you yourself find less interesting may appeal to some or all of your students.

The time needed for basic work (reading and Student's Book exercises) will vary slightly from one unit to the next. This is because of the varying length and difficulty of the texts and, more importantly, because different texts lend themselves to different kinds of exercises. It is a good idea to take a look at the unit you plan to use before going into the classroom: You are the best judge of your students' abilities. However, 40 minutes is the average time a typical unit will take. If you want to spend less time than this, you might consider doing the *Summary skills* exercise in class and assigning some or all of the other exercises for homework.

Warm-up, or getting students thinking about the topic of the text they are about to read, is an important part of the reading comprehension lesson. In the classroom we are trying to prepare students for the reading they will do outside of it; and in their normal lives they will not usually be approaching a text "cold," without any idea of what it is about. The Student's Book contains a short introduction to each text, which places it in its context; but in addition the Teacher's Manual provides suggestions for brief sensitization exercises to use before students open their books.

Summary skills exercises are an important feature of *Genuine Articles*. The reasons for their prominence were explained previously. Account has been taken of the different ways people have of organizing their perceptions, and different modes of thinking are called for from one unit to the next.

In order for your students to get the full benefit of the *Summary skills* exercises, they should feel free to look back at the texts as they do them. This exercise is printed facing the text in most units, and there are frequent suggestions that students refer back to the text. But you will probably have to remind them often that they can do so; it will ultimately be your attitude as a teacher that determines the students' success or failure in this area.

The other exercises that follow the text are not exactly the same in every unit. Each set of exercises helps students deal with the particular difficulties of the text it follows and trains them to cope with similarly constructed texts in the future. You will also find that some types of exercise recur more frequently than others. This is because the skills involved are needed more frequently or are more difficult to assimilate. Here is a list of the exercise types and titles you will find in the Student's Book.

1. *Summary skills.* Also called *Do you have the main ideas?* and *Getting the picture.*
2. *Guessing words from context.* This very useful skill is practiced with low-frequency words, because these are the ones students are least likely to know already. You may want to point out that it is the skills, and not the words, that you intend for them to learn from the exercises.
3. *Reading for specific information.* This helps with so-called scanning skills.
4. *Inference.* This exercise helps students learn to make inferences properly and to avoid making false inferences. Also called *How will it continue?, Opinions and feelings, Attitudes and feelings, How good is your picture?*

5. *Making connections.* This exercise type includes making logical connections between the different parts of a text and recognizing such things as the antecedents of pronouns (sometimes referred to as anaphora). Similar exercises are also called *Vocabulary links, Why?,* and *Why and how?*
6. *Reading carefully for details.* This helps students overcome difficulties linked to reading complicated sentences, reading details carelessly, missing negative expressions. Similar exercises are also called *Facts and figures.*

The Teacher's Manual gives notes on dealing with the individual exercises, as well as a key to the answers. You should be encouraged, rather than dismayed, if most of your students get most of the answers right: This is an indication that the book is at the correct level for your class. The important thing in improving students' reading skills is the work involved in doing each exercise; the answers to the questions are merely a by-product of this work.

Working in groups or pairs is one implication of this attitude to the exercises. It is sometimes easier for students to accept and adopt a way of approaching a problem if the suggestion comes from another student, rather than from the teacher. Group work also gives each student more time to be actively involved in classroom interaction and allows the teacher to help with individual problems without stopping the entire class. Of course, you will not be able to hear everything that is said, or correct every mistake as soon as it is made. But you will be able to hear and correct as much as you would in a traditional class, and you will gain the extra advantages mentioned previously.

A few of the exercises in the Student's Book specifically suggest working in groups; most of the others are very well suited to this way of learning. Three ways to organize group work are:
1. Groups of three to five people do the exercise together. Each group can then report to the class if you have the time and judge that this is useful.
2. Each person does the exercise individually. Small groups are formed, answers are compared, and a consensus is reached in each group. Each group can then report to the class if you wish.
3. Begin in the same way as 1 or 2, but after the small-group work, one person leaves each group to report to one of the other groups. This is appropriate for exercises where you expect a variety of answers.

Additional activities

Genuine Articles is designed primarily to improve reading comprehension skills. But if you want to use the theme of the reading comprehension lesson as the basis for other classroom activities, the notes in this book will give you detailed guidance on how to do so. For each unit you will find suggestions for:

– *Oral fluency practice.* This is an activity in which students approach the topic of the reading passage from an entirely different viewpoint. Besides giving them a specific framework in which to practice their speaking skills, this encourages the activation of passive vocabulary encountered in the text. There is a great deal of variation in the form of these activities: Students are asked to organize discussions, carry out role play, conduct class surveys, engage in brainstorming sessions, agree with another student on a detailed plan, and so on.

— *Vocabulary work.* This section calls on students to choose a few words from the text to learn. Learning will be much more effective if the students do choose the words themselves. Studies on "cognitive depth"* indicate that students will remember words better if they are made to think about their reasons for choosing them. It is necessary to use a dictionary for this activity; at this level students should be using a good learner's dictionary in English rather than a translating dictionary. Try and make sure that they have, or have access to, the *Longman Dictionary of American English* or the *Oxford Student's Dictionary of American English.*

— *Writing practice.* This section provides opportunities for students to use the patterns from the text in a short piece of personal writing. If you give some of these activities for homework, you may want to adopt the following system in order to give students an extra learning opportunity: When you mark homework, instead of writing in the correct words when there is a mistake, write an abbreviation (e.g., *sp* for spelling mistakes, *v* for a mistake in the verb form) according to a code you have given the students. Then hand the homework back and let the students have a try at correcting their own mistakes. You can then do the final correction yourself; or you can add another stage where students work in pairs to help one another. You might even want to copy the different pieces of homework and distribute them to small groups so they can work together.

*Fergus I. M. Craik, "A levels of analysis view of memory." In Patricia Pliner, L. Krames, and T. Alloway (eds.), *Communication and Affect: Language and Thought* (New York: Academic Press, 1973). For an excellent discussion of memory and language learning, see E. Stevick, *Memory, Meaning and Method: Some Psychological Perspectives on Language Learning* (Rowley, Mass: Newbury House, 1976).

Part 1   Instructions: How to do things

1   How to shine at a job interview

Warm-up

Ask students to vote by a show of hands on the following question: What is the most important factor in getting a job – qualifications, an impressive résumé, or the job interview? When students have voted, ask them to divide into groups of three or four and tell one another the reasons for their votes.

Many of the words and phrases in this text may be unknown to your students. You might want to explain that one of the aims of the book is to help students get information from texts without having to know every single word. Ask them to read the text carefully, as many times as they want, but not to worry too much about words they do not know.

Do you have the main ideas?

Doing this exercise will probably involve reading most of the text again. Have students compare answers with one another, to see where the problems are. Then discuss the answers with the entire class.

Answers: The important points are numbers 2, 4, 5, and 6.

Guessing words from context

You can use the correction of this exercise as a learning activity by discussing any wrong answers with the class, and helping them see why those answers are wrong.

Answers: 1j, 2e, 3i, 4k, 5l, 6a, 7h, 8d

How will it continue?

This is a good exercise to do in small groups, as it will provoke discussion. The sentences that might be used to continue the article are numbers 2, 4, and 5. (Not 1 because it contradicts what is said under Myth 4; not 3 because "making a good impression" contradicts the advice under Myth 2; not 6 because of the constant advice to be yourself and be honest.)

ADDITIONAL ACTIVITIES

Hiring an employee

This exercise takes some preparation. Collect several help-wanted ads from newspapers. English-language newspapers are best, of course, but if there are none available use advertisements in the students' native language. In this case you may have to supply some vocabulary. You should try to get a wide range of advertisements – some that students might really apply for and some you know will be "dream" jobs for them. If you have a large number of students in the class, you may wish to have more than one copy of the same ad.

Divide the students into groups of five or six and pass the ads around. Each student selects an ad. The students take turns reading their ad aloud and being interviewed for the job by the other members of the group.

Vocabulary work

Ask each stuent to choose four or five words or phrases from the text to learn. Students should look the words up in a dictionary, and find out from the dictionary or from you whether the words would be acceptable to use in a business letter. They should then write two appropriate sentences with each word, indicating in what context the sentences might be found.

Writing practice

1. Students who want or need practice in writing letters could write a letter of application for one of the jobs in the *Hiring an employee* exercise, or for another job that they could choose themselves.
2. Assuming that a North American would approach a job interview according to the advice in the article, students could write a letter of advice to an imaginary North American friend. The letter would outline the changes the North American should make in his or her interview technique in order to adapt to customs in the student's own country.

---

2   How to protect yourself

Warm-up

Before students open their books, ask if anyone in the class has ever had a burglary at home, or had a pocket or purse picked. If so, ask if the victim would tell the others about the experience. If not, ask them how they think they would feel and what they think they would do if they came home one day and found their home in a complete mess and half of their belongings gone.

Then have them read the text, taking as much time as they want and reading it more than once if they would like to. Tell them not to worry about words they cannot understand as long as they can get the general meaning of the passage.

Summary skills

Students could do this exercise in pairs or small groups. Walk around the room while they are working to give any help that is needed.

Answers: a5, b2, c6, d1, e4, f9, g3

Guessing words from context

Let students do the exercise individually and then compare answers in small groups before checking with you. Answers:

1. forced
2. obscured
3. secure
4. high shrubbery / bushes
5. peephole
6. credentials
7. lobby
8. call
9. engrave
10. bogus

Making connections

It would be a good idea to let the students compare their answers in pairs or small groups once they have attempted the exercise individually. Answers:

1. a side drive or garage
2. a delivery or serviceman
3. a suspicious-looking person in your lobby
4. a repairman
5. a friend
6. your driver's license or other identifying number

Why?

This exercise is more challenging and requires students to infer information implicit in the text or to use their knowledge of the world to think about the text. It is best to do it in small groups. You will probably want to walk around while the students are working to give any help they need. Answers (in these or in other words):

1. So that burglars cannot hide in the dark places.
2. They may only be pretending to be deliverymen in order to get into your house.
3. The person might force you to let him or her into your apartment. / The person might rob you in the lobby.
4. Burglars are less likely to enter a home if they think someone is there.
5. To prove you are the owner. If they are stolen and the police find them they can return them to you.
6. People could phone to see if you are home and come to your home while you are out to burglarize it.

ADDITIONAL ACTIVITIES

Discussion

Divide the class into groups of four or five (a group can have only three people in it, but this is not so satisfactory). In this exercise, five points will be discussed. Each student will have responsibility for one or more points, making sure that all the other members of the group express themselves on that point, and taking brief notes on the opinions expressed.

3

Distribute the points for discussion, either by giving each group an envelope you have prepared, with the five points written on separate slips of paper, or by assigning numbers 1 to 5 to the students and then writing the numbered points on the board. Students will probably work better if you give them a realistic time limit for this exercise. Here are the points:

1. Give at least one practical suggestion on how the general public could be made more aware of how homes could be protected from burglary.
2. In some countries, insurance companies will not pay for a burglary if it can be shown that the house was not locked. Is this fair? Is it useful?
3. In some cases in the United States, criminals are not only being sentenced to prison, but are also being held financially responsible if they injure someone. What do you think of this?
4. Do you think it is safe, in the city where you are now, for a woman to walk alone in the street at night?
5. In the United States, there are separate local telephone numbers for the fire department, the police department, and ambulances. In some cities there is also a single number (911) that you can dial for any emergency. What are the advantages and disadvantages of each system?

You can always let the students run over the time limit if all the discussions are going well; but setting a limit does seem to keep the discussions moving. As the groups discuss, walk around the classroom to give help to students who ask for it. It is better not to correct students' English at this point; you may want to note down for yourself any mistakes that come up often, so you can deal with them in another class. The important thing is that the students communicate with one another in English.

If a group finishes early, they can listen to a neighboring group.

Vocabulary work

Have students choose four or five words or expressions from the text that they do not ordinarily use when speaking or writing English. The students should look the words up in an English dictionary and write two sentences using each one.

Writing practice

The aim of this exercise is to give students practice in writing instructions, while allowing them to use their imagination and sense of humor. Working in groups, students are to write out sets of instructions for tourists coming to the country where the class is. These instructions should be completely false and designed to get the tourists into the maximum amount of trouble. For example:

TIPPING ON BUSES
Always give a small tip (a nickel or dime) to the driver of the bus when you buy your ticket or pay your fare. Put the money discreetly into one of the uniform pockets.

Ask the students to number their instructions and give a brief title to each one. You may have to ask the class as a whole for a few more examples before they begin working, to make sure everyone has gotten the idea.

3   How to save a life

Warm-up

Before the students open their books, ask them what the dangers of swimming alone are and what they would do if they saw someone drowning. Get them to describe what they would do once they got the person out of the water. Help them with any vocabulary they need.

Then have them read the text. Make sure they know they can read it more than once and take as much time as they need. (For a listening exercise on this same topic, see Unit 15 in *Listening Tasks* by Sandra Schecter, Cambridge University Press.)

Summary skills 1

Let the students work individually on this exercise before comparing answers in small groups. Remind them that they can look back at the text as often as they wish. The correct chart is shown in Figure 3.1.

Summary skills 2

This exercise should not take long. Have students work in groups of two to four and agree on their answers before checking with you. The correct order is: b, d, a, c.

Guessing words from context

Get students to do the exercise individually. Then you can use the correction of the exercise as a learning activity by examining with the class any wrong answers and helping them see why those answers are wrong.
   Answers: 1h, 2c, 3e, 4b, 5j, 6l, 7k, 8f, 9d

Vocabulary links

The aim of this exercise is to show how meaning is structured in the text by the use of words that repeat ideas already mentioned.
   The exercise is best done in groups of three or four students. You may want to walk around the classroom while the students are working to give any help that is needed. Answers:
1. casualty, patient
2. throat, mouth, nose (any two are acceptable)
3. scooping out, blotting up, clearing

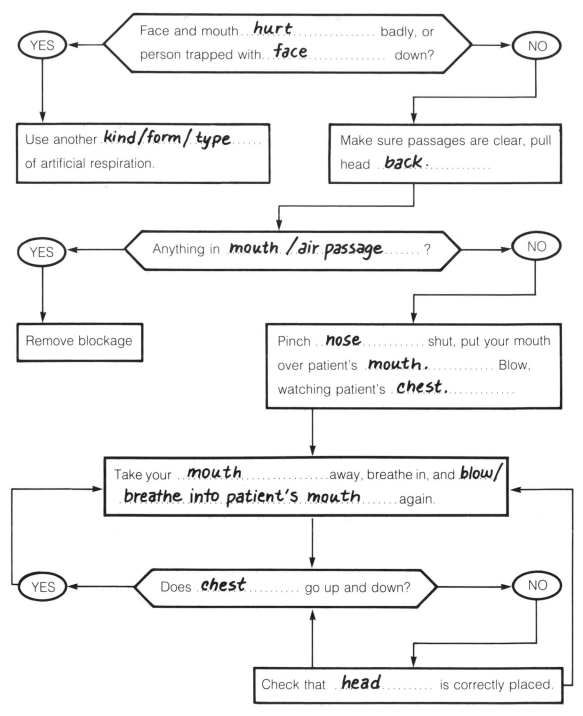

Face and mouth.. *hurt* .... badly, or person trapped with.. *face* .... down? — YES / NO

YES → Use another .*kind/form/type*...... of artificial respiration.

NO → Make sure passages are clear, pull head .*back* ....

Anything in .*mouth /air passage* .... ? — YES / NO

YES → Remove blockage

NO → Pinch ..*nose* .... shut, put your mouth over patient's .*mouth.* .... Blow, watching patient's .*chest.* ....

Take your .*mouth* ....away, breathe in, and *blow/* .*breathe into patient's mouth* ......again.

Does .*chest* .... go up and down? — YES / NO

NO → Check that .*head* .... is correctly placed.

Figure 3.1

4. jaw, teeth, tongue, nose (any two are acceptable)
5. breathe, expel air

ADDITIONAL ACTIVITIES

Oral instructions

Divide the class into pairs (one group of three is all right). Each person thinks of an action for his or her partner to mime, for example, typing, climbing a ladder, driving a car. Then, *without saying what the action is,* one partner instructs the other how to place and move the different parts of the body in order to mime the action. The actor must guess the action and then has a turn at giving instructions. Pairs who finish early can find new partners and start again.

Vocabulary work

Ask students to choose four or five words or expressions from the text that they think would be useful in writing instructions. Have them explain the reason for their choice to another student. Then ask them to write two sentences using each word or expression.

Writing practice

Ask students to write one of the following sets of instructions. They should try to be as clear and comprehensive as they can. They can draw diagrams if they want.
1. Write instructions for foreign tourists in your country, telling them exactly how to use a public telephone to call a number in the United States or Canada. Include details of what to do if there is a problem with the call.
2. Imagine you are going to lend your car to someone. Write precise instructions on how to start the car and use the various accessories (lights, windshield wipers, etc.).
3. Write instructions for foreign tourists in your country, telling them what steps to follow if their money and papers are stolen.
4. Write down a recipe for someone who has never seen you prepare the dish.

---

4   How to win at marriage

Warm-up

Before students open their books, you may want to give them a short warm-up period. Ask them to think of as many things as they can that cause disagreement between the two members of a couple. You might want to list them on the board under the headings "Big things" and "Small things."

Then make sure they understand they are to read the text carefully and can read it more than once. Tell them not to worry too much about words they don't understand, as long as they get the general meaning.

Summary skills

As with most of the exercises, it is useful to let students compare answers with one another in small groups, once they have done the exercises individually. Answers:

1. Don't
2. Do
3. Don't
4. Do
5. Do
6. Don't
7. Don't
8. Do
9. Do
10. Don't
11. Don't
12. Don't
13. Don't

Guessing words from context

Do not expect the students to explain how they arrived at the answers to the last three questions: Different people may have different valid ways of getting to the answers, and they may not always be able to say how they did it. If one answer gives particular trouble, however, you may want to show how it can be deduced.

Accept answers that can be legitimately deduced from the text, but are not exact definitions of the words. For example, *requiring* in question 8 can be thought to mean *asking for* or *expecting* rather than *needing*. You may then want to tell students what the exact meaning is or refer them to their dictionaries. Answers (in these or different words):

1. hesitate / think it's wrong
2. pleased / glad / happy
3. bad
4. bad
5. come to an end slowly
6. now
7. problem
8. asking for / expecting / needing

Vocabulary links

This exercise is different from the *Guessing words from context* exercise that precedes it. Your students will certainly know the italicized words in the questions. The aim of the exercise is not, therefore, to help them guess these words, but to show how meaning is structured in the passage by the use of words that repeat previously mentioned ideas.

The exercise is best done in groups of three or four students. You may want to walk around the classroom while they are working to give any help that is needed. Answers:

1. nothing, small
2. kids, friends, relatives (*presence* is also a correct answer)
3. calm, measured (mean the same); histrionic, irritated (mean the opposite)
4. hit, slaps

How will it continue?

This exercise gives students practice in making the inferences the author intended them to make. It is a good exercise to do in small groups, as it will provoke discussion. The sentences that might be in the rest of the article are numbers 1, 2, and 4. (Not number 3 because this could involve putting off fights indefinitely, and the author stresses the importance of fighting about anything that comes up, even small things; not number 5 because the author says not to apologize, but to carry on and "start somewhere else, on something new.")

ADDITIONAL ACTIVITIES

Class survey

In this exercise, each student is assigned one of the questions given here. Ask each student to interview as many of the other class members as possible in 15 minutes, and then write a very short report on the findings of the survey and present it to the class. Fifteen questions are given here. If there are more than 15 people in your class, you can give the same question to more than one person and tell them to compare their answers before giving a joint report. If you have a very small class, you may want to give each person more than one question. Omit any questions that are not appropriate for your class, for example, number 15 if you think that few students have had enough exposure to North Americans to have an opinion on it.

1. Do you ever scream and yell at people?
2. How reasonable are you when you disagree with somebody: very reasonable, fairly reasonable, not very reasonable, it depends on the person?
3. Do you think about an argument for a long time after it's finished, or do you forget it quickly?
4. Who is the person you disagree with most often? (Name their relationship to you: friend, parent, etc.)
5. Do you argue (fight) very often?
6. How often do you get really angry: once a week, once a month, once a year, ... ?
7. Have you ever hit someone in anger?
8. Do you agree with the author of the text that it is good to fight occasionally?
9. Do you find it easy to apologize: always / usually / sometimes / never?
10. Can you remember your parents arguing in front of you when you were small?

11. What would you do if you had a married couple at your home for dinner and they began fighting at the dinner table?
12. Who do you think gets angry more often, men or women?
13. What would upset you more: to see two men or two women yelling and screaming at one another in a restaurant?
14. What would you do if you were taking care of two children, seven and eight years old, and they began fighting?
15. Do North Americans seem to get angry more often or less often than people in your country?

Vocabulary work

Have each student choose five unfamiliar words from the text and look them up in a dictionary. The student should find out (perhaps from you) which words could be used in a formal situation, like a statement to the police, and write sentences using each word in an appropriate context.

Writing practice

Have students write advice for North Americans coming to their country (or countries) titled "How to win at work" or "How to win at school."

Part 2   Descriptions: What things are like

5   Athens is dying

Warm-up

To introduce the theme of this article, ask students to show by raising their hands which of them would rather live in the city and which would rather live in the country. One or two students could give reasons for their choice.

Then have them read the text, taking as much time as they want and reading it more than once if they would like to.

Summary skills

This exercise gives students the opportunity to choose for themselves which aspect of the text they want to focus on. Have them do the exercise individually first; then ask each student to find at least one other person who has chosen the same topic. Answers will vary somewhat, but the students' final notes should look something like this:

1. AIR POLLUTION
   – smog hurts eyes and chokes senses
   – sulfur dioxide eats marble on Acropolis
   – 180–300 mg of sulfur dioxide per cubic meter of air (4 times what WHO thinks safe)
   – nearly half pollution from cars
   – few parks and few oxygen-producing plants

2. OVERCROWDING
   – buses jam crowded streets
   – inadequate sewerage facilities
   – cannot expand: hemmed in by mountains, sea; 135 sq. mi., 3.7 million people
   – 120,000 move from provinces to Athens per year (40% of Greeks in Athens)
   – by year 2000: 6.5 million in Athens (½ Greece's population)
   – save-Athens ministry proposing taxes against in-migration, projects to keep people in countryside, moving government offices to city's fringes

3. TRAFFIC
   – rush hour horrible
   – Athens built without plan
   – poor public transport
   – cars cause half of pollution of air
   – high prices for cars and fuel don't discourage people from driving
   – save-Athens ministry moving many government offices to city's fringes (may improve traffic conditions in center?)

Guessing words from context

Answers (in these or other words):

1. not having
2. crowded, pushed together
3. left
4. have, face
5. a long time
6. move
7. begun

Facts and figures

Notice that the answers to these questions are not found directly in the text. The students must use the figures in the text and do simple calculations to arrive at the answers.

1.

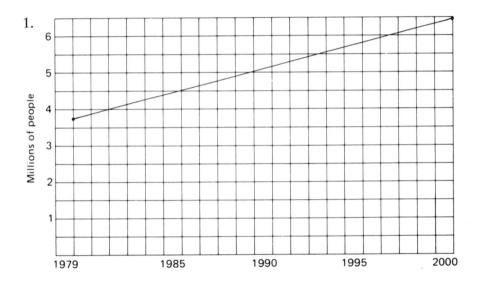

2. 36,000 (3,000 per month × 12 months)
3. 27,407 (3,700,000 people ÷ 135 square miles)
4. 9,250,000 (3.7 million people in Athens ÷ .40 of Greece's population)
5. 75 mg of sulfur dioxide per cubic meter (300 mg ÷ 4 times safe level)

ADDITIONAL ACTIVITIES

Brainstorming

This activity is best done in small groups of about five people. Each group chooses one of the problems of Athens:

— noise
— air pollution
— overcrowding
— poor public transport

The group then has three tasks:

1. The brainstorming itself. During this time the members of the group try to think of as many ways as possible to help solve their problem. One group member should act as secretary and write all the ideas down. Any idea, no matter how nonsensical it seems, should be expressed: It is quantity, not quality, that matters at this stage. A seemingly ridiculous idea can sometimes spur a creative and practical one. You might want to give a time limit to this part of the exercise.
2. Feasibility rating. The group should give each idea a feasibility rating; from 1 for an easy-to-carry-out, inexpensive project to 4 for an almost impossible idea.
3. Effectiveness rating. The group should take the ten or so most feasible ideas and rate them according to how far they will go toward solving the problem: **A** for a very effective idea, **B** for an effective idea, etc.

You may want the groups to report their findings to the class when they have finished, but this is a case where the process is more important than the product, and the reporting can easily be dropped.

Vocabulary work

Students should each choose five words or so from the text to learn. They should look the words up in a dictionary and also find out (perhaps from you) whether their words could be used in a scientific report or whether they are too informal or emotive for that use. They should write a sentence or two using each word.

Writing practice

Ask students to describe their own or another city / town / village, using the article as a model.

6   Zen and the art of motorcycle maintenance

Warm-up

To introduce students to the theme of the text, you could begin by asking them to tell you as many ways of traveling as they can think of. Write the ways on the board as they tell you. Then go back over the list and ask students to vote by a show of hands for their favorite way of traveling.

Summary skills

Make sure students understand what they are to do before they begin. They can compare answers in small groups once they have done the exercise individually. Answers (in these or other words):

Summary 1

The narrator is traveling across an area of the ~~Rocky Mountains~~ **Central Plains** by motorcycle. It is a hot, ~~dry~~ **muggy** morning, and there are a lot of ~~hills~~ **marshes** along the ~~new~~ **old** highway the narrator is using. The air from the marshes is ~~warm~~ **cool**.

Summary 2

This ~~is~~ **isn't** the first time the narrator has been in this country. He is ~~un~~happy to be back in this ~~irritating~~ **relaxing** place and see the plants and animals again. His son, Chris, who is riding ~~beside~~ **behind** him on ~~another~~ **the same** cycle, ~~is~~ **isn't** impressed with the bird his dad notices.

Summary 3

Chris is 11; the narrator thinks that is too ~~old~~ **young** to be impressed with blackbirds. The blackbird is interesting to the narrator because it reminds him of ~~a story~~ **memories** he ~~read~~ **has**: ~~deer~~ **duck** hunting in the marshes in the autumn, walking ~~through~~ **across** the ~~mud~~ **ice and snow** in the winter.

Summary 4

Traveling on a motorcycle is ~~not so good as~~ **better than** traveling by car, because on a motorcycle you are a participant rather than a spectator. You ~~can~~ **can't** ignore the experience of traveling. The narrator and his son have very ~~definite~~ **indefinite** plans about their vacation, because it is the ~~destination~~ **traveling** that interests them more than the ~~journey~~ **destination**.

Do you have the main ideas?

This exercise will provoke a lot of discussion in the class, so it is probably most usefully done in small groups. You can walk around to give students any help they need. When the groups have finished you can discuss the answers with the class as a whole, getting students to tell you why the wrong answers are wrong.

Answers: the scenery, the narrator's past experience of this place, the pleasure and interest of traveling by motorcycle.

Guessing words from context

This would be a good exercise to do in pairs or small groups. Answers:

1. slough
2. two-laner
3. humid / muggy
4. cattails
5. bump
6. muck
7. helmet
8. hollers
9. focus
10. whizzing
11. overwhelming

ADDITIONAL ACTIVITIES

Vacation survey

In this exercise, each student is assigned one of the questions given here. Ask each student to interview as many of the other class members as possible in 15 minutes, and then write a very short report on the findings of the survey and present it to the class. Fifteen questions are given here. If there are more than 15 people in your class, you can give the same question to more than one person and tell them to compare their answers before giving a joint report. Omit any questions that are not appropriate for your class, for example, number 9 if you think that very few people in the class have been on an airplane.

1. On vacation, do you prefer staying in one place or traveling around? Why?
2. Do you enjoy camping, or would you like to go camping? Why?
3. Do you / would you enjoy riding a motorcycle? Why?
4. Do you prefer traveling on freeways and turnpikes, or on smaller roads? Why?
5. Have you ever spent your vacation hiking? Would you like to do it (again)?
6. What sports do you enjoy on vacation? Do you play any sports all year round?
7. Have you ever been abroad on vacation? Where?
8. Would you rather go on vacation to an exciting foreign city or to some beautiful mountain / seaside / hilly place in your own country? Why?
9. Do you enjoy being in an airplane or not?
10. Would you like to take a cruise around the world on an ocean liner? Why?
11. What country in the world would you like to visit most?
12. Have you ever hitchhiked? Would you like to do it (again)?
13. Do you / would you enjoy traveling alone? Why?
14. What is your main reason for going on vacation?
15. Do you / would you enjoy going on a package trip where everything is planned for you? Why?

Vocabulary work

Have students choose four or five words or expressions to learn from the text. They should look the words up in the dictionary, and find out from you whether the words are used only in a familiar style. They should use the words in sentences, possibly in the writing exercise that follows.

Writing practice

You could give students a choice between these two tasks:
1. Reread lines 34–49. Then write a description of your memories of a place and the things you did there.
2. Reread lines 50–65. Then write a description of some sport or pastime you enjoy. A person who isn't familiar with the activity should be able to tell from the description why you enjoy it.

---

7   Vacationing in Mexico

Warm-up

Ask students to imagine they have just won a two-week vacation for two in Mexico. Get volunteers to tell you how they would spend their two weeks.

Alternatively, you may want to change the procedure in this unit and have the students do the *Reading for specific information* exercise before reading the text straight through. Often when we read a text we are trying only to extract those bits of information that are useful to us rather than to get a detailed picture of the entire passage. *Reading for specific information* practices this skill.

Getting the picture

Careful reading of the text will give students the clues they need to name the numbered places on the map. Let them work individually for a while and then compare answers in small groups. If they are having trouble, you may want to point out the ferry line between numbers 2 and 4 and the sailfish near number 6. Answers:
1. Kino Bay
2. Topolobampo
3. Los Mochis
4. La Paz
5. Cabo San Lucas
6. Mazatlán

Reading for specific information

Once students have done this exercise individually, it would be useful for them to compare answers in small groups before you discuss the answers with the entire class. Answers:
1. Mazatlán
2. Mazatlán; you could also accept La Paz, San José del Cabo, and Cabo San Lucas, although no airport is mentioned.
3. Los Mochis
4. Baja California
5. Puerto Vallarta

Guessing words from context

When you are correcting this exercise, find out what wrong answers were given and discuss why they were wrong. This will help students the next time they need to guess unknown words.

Answers: 1i, 2f, 3a, 4d, 5h, 6j, 7b, 8g

ADDITIONAL ACTIVITIES

Planning a vacation

Students should choose two places from the text – places where they would enjoy spending a vacation. Then have them walk around the classroom, each trying to find another student who has chosen at least one of the same places. The pair should decide on one place for their vacation, discuss the reasons for their choice, and decide when they would like to go and how long they would like to stay.

Vocabulary work

Ask students to choose from the text four or five adjectives that are used to make the places sound attractive. Have them look words up in a dictionary. Then they should write a sentence or two using each one, or try to use them in the *Writing practice* exercise.

Writing practice

Ask students to write two short place descriptions like the ones in the text. They can describe the place where they live, places where they have been, or places they would like to go, trying to make them sound as appealing as possible.

8 Men of the Pine Barrens

Warm-up

Before students open their books, ask them to show by raising their hands which of them would like to spend a year in a very isolated place without many neighbors, living by themselves. Ask a few of the more extroverted students to give reasons for their choice.

Then have them read the text, taking as much time as they want and stopping when they like.

Reading for specific information

This is a good exercise to do in pairs or threes. Make sure the students understand they only have to write brief notes in each space. The completed table might look something like this:

	Fred Brown	*The young man*
age	79; looks 60 (lines 27–29)	doesn't say
hair	short, bristly, white (line 24)	long, black (line 33)
eyes	bright, fast-moving (line 25)	looking past his feet, staring (lines 40–41)
face	wide-open (line 25)	tanned, gaunt (line 46)
shirt	white, sleeveless (lines 8–9)	coarse-woven, V neck (lines 35–36)
trousers	none (undershorts) (line 9)	canvas (line 37)
legs	trim, strong, large muscles in calves (lines 26–27)	stretched out, one ankle over the other (line 39)
shoes	ankle-top shoes (line 9)	gum boots (= rubber boots) (line 38)
personality	cheerful / friendly (line 10)	shy / quiet (line 49)

Guessing words from context

Get students to do the exercise individually. Then you can use the correction of the exercise as a learning activity by examining with the class any wrong answers and helping them see why those answers are wrong.

Answers: 1j, 2c, 3e, 4h, 5i, 6k, 7b, 8f, 9d

Inference

This is a more challenging exercise; it is best done in small groups so the students can pool resources. Answers:

1. It must be warm, since Fred Brown is wearing a sleeveless shirt and undershorts.
2. Probably not, since Fred calls out to the narrator to come on into the house.
3. Probably not, as he is 79; and he does not seem to be worried about having gotten up late.
4. Yes, because he has trim, strong legs with very muscular calves.
5. From his clothes (cap and boots) and his tan, he probably works outdoors.
6. Probably the young man, as he is completely dressed, while Fred is still in his shorts and eating breakfast.

ADDITIONAL ACTIVITIES

Discussion

Divide the class into groups of four or five (a group can have only three people in it, but this is not so satisfactory). In this exercise, five points will be discussed. Each student will have the responsibility for one or more points, making sure that all the other members of the group express themselves and taking brief notes on the opinions expressed.

Distribute the points for discussion, either by giving each group an envelope you have prepared, with the five points written on separate slips of paper, or by assigning numbers 1 to 5 to the students and then writing the numbered points on the board. Students will probably work better if you give them a realistic time limit for this exercise. Here are the points:
1. Do you think Fred Brown is lonely? Why?
2. Do you think the young man is lonely? Why?
3. Do you feel more sympathetic toward Fred Brown or the young man? Why?
4. What has been the loneliest time of your life?
5. Would you / do you like to live alone? Why?

You can always let the students run over the time limit if all discussions are going well; but setting a time limit does seem to keep the discussions moving. As the groups discuss, walk around the classroom to give help to the students who ask for it. It is better not to correct students' English at this point; you may want to note down for yourself any mistakes that come up often, so you can deal with them in another class. The important thing is that the students communicate with one another in English.

If a group finishes early, they can listen to a neighboring group.

Vocabulary work

Ask each student to choose about four words from the text to learn and to tell another student why these words were chosen. After looking up the words in a dictionary, the student should write a sentence or two with each word.

Writing practice

Students should each write a short description of a person, situating the character in his or her environment (home, work, school). This can be a person the student knows, a fictional character, or someone from a picture in a magazine.

Part 3   Processes: How things happen

9 Power

Warm-up

Before students open their books, get them thinking about the theme of the text by asking them to name some powerful people. Write the names on the board as they give them to you. When you have about ten names, ask them to choose the three most powerful.

Reading for specific information

Before students read the text, get them to look at the table and ask you about any unfamiliar vocabulary. Then tell them to try to complete the table as quickly as possible by looking at the article.

Once students have done the exercise individually, let them compare answers in small groups before checking with you. The completed table:

	People who need and have power	People who need power but don't have it
Mentally healthy	Yes (lines 30–32)	No (lines 25–28)
Depressed	No (lines 39–41)	Yes (lines 33–36)
Sexually satisfied	Yes (lines 42–47)	No (lines 42–47)
Self-assured	No (lines 48–53)	No (lines 48–53)
Good judges of sincerity	No (lines 52–53)	No (lines 52–53)
Loyal friends	No (lines 61–62)	No (lines 61–65)
Attractive to the opposite sex	Men – yes; women – no (lines 66–75)	Men – less; women – DS (lines 70–73)
Wise	No (lines 76–84)	No (lines 76–84)

Have them read the text, taking as long as they want and stopping as often as they like.

Guessing words from context

The correction of this exercise can be a learning activity if you find out what wrong answers were chosen and help students see why they were wrong. Answers:

1. short-range
2. status
3. lift
4. dismiss
5. weapon
6. peoples
7. fulfilled

Reading carefully for details

The "doesn't say" feature of this exercise is designed to make students read more carefully and avoid making unwarranted inferences.
  Answers: 1F, 2F, 3T, 4DS, 5T, 6T

ADDITIONAL ACTIVITIES

Drafting a constitution

Divide the students into groups of four or five, and give them the following task:

Imagine your country has been a colony and will be independent in a year's time. You are the committee that has been appointed to write a constitution for the new country. You must decide how to divide the power between the President, the Legislature, and the Supreme Court. Try to make sure none of them has too much power. Here are some of the questions you must think about:
1. How long will each official hold office? Will the official be elected or appointed? By whom?
2. Who makes the laws? Can anybody veto the laws? Can the veto be overturned?
3. Who proposes the budget, and who approves it?
4. Can anyone dissolve the legislature? Can anyone dismiss the president? Can anyone dismiss the Supreme Court judges?
5. Can anyone change the constitution? Who decides if a new law agrees with the constitution?
6. Whose job is it to make sure the laws are obeyed? What powers are available for this?
7. Who controls the army, navy, and air force? Who can declare war?
  It is probably best to give students a time limit for this task; if things are going very well in all the groups you can let them go over the limit, but it will give them something to work toward. If there is time when they have finished, the different groups can compare their results.

Vocabulary work

Ask students to choose three new words or expressions from the text that they would use in a letter to a friend, and two new words or expressions that they would use in a business letter. You could have them check with you if their dictionaries do not give adequate information on this point. Once they have checked and looked the words up in the dictionary, they should write one or two sentences with each word.

Writing practice

Ask students to write about processes they are familiar with. The processes they choose will depend on their own backgrounds. For example, they might write about how a car works, how scholarships are granted, how a certain holiday is celebrated, or how people deal with the death of someone they love. They should use the same "quiz" format as the text, but shorten it by dealing with only three or four points.

10   Smoke signals

Warm-up

Before the students open their books, introduce the theme of the text by saying: "Some fires start accidentally and some are started on purpose. What sort of person do you think starts fires on purpose, and what do you think should be done about it?"

   Then let them read the text, as slowly and as many times as they want.

Summary skills

Let students work together in groups of two to four to pool their resources for this exercise. The missing labels (in these or other words):
1. Personal problem
2. Boy starts fires
6. Bond is created
7. Boy stops setting fires

Guessing words from context

Let students complete the exercise individually and then compare answers in groups before checking with you. Use the correction of the exercise to examine any wrong answers, and help the students see why they are wrong.
   Answers: 1n, 2k, 3e, 4b, 5m, 6i, 7g, 8l, 9a, 10q

Vocabulary links

The aim of this exercise is to help students see how meaning is structured in the passage by the use of words that are related to one another. Ask students to work in groups of two or three and to agree on answers before checking with you. Answers:
1. youngster
2. guidance, friendly
3. relation, charges, get-together, care about
4. worried

Why?

This exercise requires students to search for the logical links in the text.
Answers (in these or other words):
1. The boys were trying to say that they needed help.
2. To find firemen to participate in the program.
3. To make them realize how serious it is to start fires.
4. So the boys realize someone cares for them; then perhaps they will stop
   setting fires. / To give them a father figure.

Inference

Have students do this exercise in groups of two to four so that they can
pool their resources. Answers:
1. Dr. Gaynor wants to keep kids out of the juvenile justice system, which
   is ready to "call them arsonists," that is, identify them as criminals. If
   they consider themselves criminals, they may act like criminals. (lines
   79–88)
2. An overweight boy tried lighting fires in the refrigerator. (lines 12–15)

ADDITIONAL ACTIVITIES

Class survey

In this exercise, each student is assigned one of the questions given here.
Ask each student to interview as many of the other class members as
possible in 15 minutes, and then write a brief report and present it to the
class. Fifteen questions are given here. If there are more than 15 people in
your class, you can give the same question to more than one person and tell
them to compare their answers before giving a joint report. If there are very
few people in the class, you may want to give each student two questions.
Omit any questions that are not appropriate for your class, for example,
the second part of question 4 if you think few or no students have cars.
   1. Have you ever had a fire in your home?
   2. Have you ever known a child who set fires?
   3. Does everyone in your family know how to leave the house if a fire
      breaks out while they are sleeping?
   4. Do you have a fire extinguisher in your house? In your car?
   5. What would you do if a child's clothes caught on fire?
   6. Do you think you could run through a wall of fire if you knew there
      was safety on the other side?
   7. Fire safety experts say: Don't take anything if the house is on fire – just
      get out. But what would you *feel* like saving if your home were on fire?
   8. Which frightens you the most – being caught in a fire, drowning, or
      falling from a great height?
   9. Suppose you could work for the fire department for two weeks a year.
      Would you enjoy it? Why?
  10. Do you think people should be held financially responsible for fire
      damage caused by neglect (for example, smoking in bed)?

11. Suppose you woke up one night and your room was filled with smoke. What would you do?
12. What would you do if you had a child who set small fires (not important enough to call the fire department)?
13. What sort of people do you think firefighters are?
14. If you had the choice between an inexpensive gas heater and a more expensive wood-burning fireplace in your living room, which would you choose?
15. Who should be paid more – a firefighter, a customs officer, or a nurse?

Vocabulary work

Ask students to choose five verbs or verb phrases from the text that they think might be useful to them in their own writing. They should look the words up in the dictionary and write one or more sentences with each, showing it in an appropriate context.

Writing practice

Students should describe some process in their own country (see examples below). They should choose a process they are familiar with so they can describe it in detail. Ask them to try to write connected prose. Some of the processes they might write about are:
– Getting into a university
– Getting medical care paid for, either by a national health program or by a private insurance company
– Getting a driver's license

---

11 Lions at work and play

Warm-up

Before students open their books, introduce the theme of the text by asking them which of these adjectives they would apply to lions: strong, energetic, brave, affectionate. You might want to write the four adjectives on the board and see how many votes each one gets. Then have the students read the texts, taking as much time as they want and stopping if they wish.

Do you have the main ideas?

Doing this exercise will probably involve reading most of the text again. Having students compare answers with one another before discussing them with the entire class is a good idea: It will not solve all the problems, but it will help students see where the problems are. Answers: The important points are numbers 1, 3, 5, 6, 8, and 9.

Guessing words from context

Let students work individually and then compare answers in small groups before checking with you. Do not expect students to explain how they arrived at the correct answers to the last five questions; different students may have different valid ways of getting to the answers, and they may not always be able to express how they did it. However, if one answer gives particular trouble, you may want to show how it can be deduced. Answers (in these or other words):
1. flying
2. faster / stronger / slimmer / braver (or any other appropriate adjective)
3. try
4. strong light
5. wake up / get up
6. animal that has been killed / dead animal
7. eat
8. waiting for an animal to kill
9. excitement

Inference

This exercise is challenging and is best done in groups so students can help one another. Answers:
1. If another animal has made a kill, they will drive it off. (lines 9–10)
2. Most kills are made at night or just before dawn. (lines 19–20)
3. Lions lie in ambush around a water hole. (lines 25–26)
4. The kill is the "exclamation point in the day-to-day existence of the lion," and they spend about 20 hours a day sleeping and resting. (lines 38–41)
5. Young lions touch faces with all the adults of the group, which is an act of bonding. The cubs play with everyone. (lines 47–50)

ADDITIONAL ACTIVITIES

Describing and guessing

If there are more than about 12 students in your class, you will probably want to divide them into groups of around six to ten for this exercise.

Give the students five minutes. During this time each student thinks of an animal and how to describe its habits. Then each student in turn describes the animal's habits to the rest of the class without giving its name. This description should be about one to two minutes long. The others must guess what animal they think it is.

Designing an animal

(You may not want to do this exercise if you have students in your class whose cultural background makes the idea of pets offensive to them.)

In groups of about five, students design the perfect animal for one of these uses:
- a pet who lives in an apartment in the city
- an animal to take mountain climbing
- a pet for a very organized person
- a pet that costs no money to keep
- a farm animal for a very dry climate

When they have finished, they describe their animal (with drawings if they wish) to the rest of the class.

Vocabulary work

Ask each student to find four or five words to learn from the text. These should be words that could be used in an article that was *not* about lions. Have them look the words up in a dictionary and write a sentence or two using each one.

Writing practice

Ask students to write two or three paragraphs describing habits. These can be a person's habits, an animal's habits, the habits of a group of people, the customs of a tribe or religious group, etc.

---

12   Burnout

Warm-up

Ask students to tell you what sorts of jobs people are likely to get frustrated and disappointed with. Write all the suggestions on the board as they come up; then ask students to vote for the three most frustrating and disappointing jobs.

Have students read the text carefully, stopping whenever they like. Remind them that it is not essential to understand every single word, as long as they get the general meaning.

Note: You may want to make sure students know what *butterfly* (line 50) means, so they can infer the meaning of *cocoon*.

Summary skills

Once students have done this exercise individually, they can compare their answers in small groups. This will probably help most of the students who have made mistakes to correct them. Then discuss the answers with the entire class.

Answers: 1k, 2j, 3e, 4i, 5a, 6c, 7f, 8g

Guessing words from context

Let students do the exercise individually and then compare answers in small groups before checking with you. Answers:
1. sophomore (line 28)
2. a glut on the market (lines 30–31)
3. the private sector (lines 31–32)
4. symptoms (line 34)
5. pep (line 38)
6. chronic (line 39)
7. abusing (line 64)
8. the bulk (line 68)
9. trivialize the problem (lines 94–95)
10. a passing fad (line 97)

Making connections

Students might do this exercise in groups of two or three. Answers:
1. burnout
2. the "cocoon phenomenon"
3. abusing parents
4. burnout
5. the problem
6. work

Why?

This exercise calls on students to use their own knowledge of the world to infer things about the text. Let students work independently before comparing answers in small groups and then checking with you. Answers:
1. They expect to be able to help the people they are working with, and change the people's lives, much more than they actually manage to.
2. People get off work at five o'clock.
3. Teenagers are busy developing their own personalities and don't usually have much consideration for the people around them – their parents least of all. OR Parents of teenagers sometimes expect them to stay children forever and are frustrated when their teenagers grow up and begin acting like adults.
4. Because, unlike the other strategies mentioned, it does not involve quitting a job or moving to a new place.

ADDITIONAL ACTIVITIES

Role play

This exercise takes a little preparation. You will have to copy the four role descriptions, below, so there are enough for all the students. Students will work in pairs; but if there is an uneven number of students, you can add an extra friend (Role 2B) to the second role play.

Give each student one role; tell students not to read one another's descriptions. While the students are reading their role descriptions, you can answer any questions they have about meaning. Remind them before they begin their conversations that some of them will be standing and some sitting. You should walk around the classroom while they are speaking, to give help to those who need it; but it is a good idea not to correct students' English at this point. Perhaps one or more pairs will want to perform their conversation for the class.

Role play 1

1A: You are a social worker. Your job has become very difficult this year. Government cuts in spending have forced an extremely successful parent education program and a youth program for teenagers to close. You feel that an increase in teenage crime in your area may result from this. But the strange thing is, you feel as much anger toward the people you should be helping as you do toward the government. You can't wait to get out of the office at 5:00 and not have to deal with people's problems anymore. You have asked your cousin out for a drink to talk about it. Begin, "I've got a really big problem I'd like to talk to you about . . . "

1B: Your favorite cousin is a social worker. You have always thought this cousin should go into business instead, because of an exceptional talent for organization. But social work has always been the most important thing in your cousin's life, and you're not sure he or she would be happy doing something else. You are having a drink together; listen to your cousin's problem and give advice.

Role play 2

2A: You have been unemployed for a year and have little hope of finding a job soon. Your wife or husband has a good job and the family's financial situation is not too bad. Since you have been out of work, you have been taking care of the house and spending more time with your two children. At first you were happy to do this, but lately you are less and less satisfied. You feel depressed most of the time and guilty about not wanting to be with your children as much as you once did. You have asked your best friend over for a cup of coffee. Talk to your friend about it. Begin, "I'm really worried about myself . . . "

2B: Your best friend has been unemployed for a year and has stayed at home taking care of the house and children. Your friend seemed very happy with this arrangement the last time you talked and was glad to have more time with the children. You have just heard about a job that seems perfect for your friend, and you are sure he or she could get it. But it involves being out of town two weeks out of three, and you are not sure your friend would want it. He or she has asked you over for a cup of coffee. Listen to the problem and give advice.

Vocabulary work

Each student should choose five words to learn from the text and tell
another student why those words will be useful. The student should then
write one or two sentences with each word.

Writing practice

Ask students to write a letter of advice to a friend who is suffering from
burnout. They should decide before they begin what the cause of the
problem is (work, home, etc.). Then they should write and reassure the
friend that the problem is not exceptional and advise on what he or she
might do.

Part 4   Narrative: What happened

13   The diamond

Warm-up

You may want to set the scene briefly before students read the text, by asking them where Johannesburg is, what the natural resources of South Africa are, and where Alexandria is.

Summary skills

Once students have done the exercise individually, they can compare answers in small groups. This will probably help most of the students who have made mistakes to correct them. Then discuss the answers with the entire class.

Answers: 1h or e, 2a, 3j, 4i, 5d, 6b

Making connections

It might be a good idea to let students compare their answers in small groups after doing this exercise individually. Answers:
1. *His father* means Ephraim's father's father (Ephraim's grandfather).
2. *This* means to cut a diamond perfectly.
3. *His* means a senior person.
4. *It* means the stone.

Inference

In correcting this exercise, it will help students if you find out which questions have been answered incorrectly and let students tell you why those answers are wrong. Answers:
1. No. (It says "brothers" but does not say how many.)
2. Yes. (They were diamond merchants.)
3. Yes. (He worked for his uncle Ben.)
4. No.
5. Yes. (His brothers and sisters married and had families.)
6. Yes. (He lived alone in the family house.)
7. Yes. (Nothing was expected of him.)
8. No. (The text speaks of one daughter, but does not say whether she was an only child.)
9. Yes. (In Alexandria.)
10. Yes. (He met her only after he had cut the diamond.)

Opinions and feelings

Again, it will help students to learn the skill practiced in this exercise if you find out where mistakes have been made and help the students to see why those answers were wrong.

Answers: 1d, 2f, 3j, 4c, 5g, 6e, 7b

ADDITIONAL ACTIVITIES

What will happen next?

Divide students into groups of about five. Their task is to write an ending for Ephraim's story. But there is a twist: They must incorporate four of these elements into their ending:
- a misunderstanding
- a car accident
- a war
- a stolen handbag
- a baby

Tell them that they only have to write down the most important facts of their ending, so that they can tell it to the rest of the class.

If you want, the class can vote on which group has produced the best ending.

Vocabulary work

There are several words in the text that are used metaphorically, or in ways that are not very familiar to students at this level. Your class has probably understood the meanings of the words, but could not necessarily use them with the meanings they have in the text.

Suggested procedure: Ask students to look at the word *brilliant*, line 5, and tell you what it means. (They will probably say something like "intelligent" or "clever.") Then ask them if they can use this word with a different meaning. (They will probably say something like "It was a day of brilliant sunshine" or "The colors were brilliant.")

Tell students that there are several other words in the text like this. Ask them, individually or in pairs or groups, to make at least two new sentences with each of these words (or any others they may find in the text):
- cut out (line 7)
- trade (line 8)
- stone (line 15)
- edge (line 22)
- closed (line 43)
- infected (line 44)

Walk around the room to answer students' questions as they work. They will probably want to ask you things like "Can you use *edge* in this way with anything besides *voice*?" (No.) "What word do I use in the sentence *The wound was infected _____ several kinds of bacteria?*" (*With*.)

You may want to ask for volunteers to read some of their sentences at the end of the exercise.

Writing practice

Ephraim's story is written in the style of a folk tale. Perhaps your students would enjoy writing down folk tales from their own country or countries. They can look back at the text to see what tenses, sentence structures, and connecting devices the author uses.

14   A gentleman thief

Warm-up

Before students open their books, ask them to vote on whether it is better, worse, or just as bad to steal a large sum of money from a bank as to steal an individual person's purse or wallet.

Summary skills

Explain that the summary skills exercise consists of a summary after every paragraph in the text. Students must correct the facts that are wrong in the summary. Make sure they understand what they are to do, and give them all the time they need to work. Let them compare answers in small groups before checking with you. (Some variation in answers is possible.)

Summary 1

Between 1970 and 1979 a ~~middle-aged businessman~~ named Josef Streit, [*young* / *thief*]
with ~~two~~ other men, drove a ~~Volkswagen~~ from one bank to another. They [*three* / *Porsche*]
stole ~~enormous~~ amounts of money from 28 Austrian banks. [*comfortable*]

Summary 2

Streit never hurt anyone, ~~but he~~ damaged the safes he opened. He was an [*or*]
artist ~~in his spare time~~. When he opened a safe, he did it ~~slowly~~ and [*at opening safes* / *quickly*]
carefully, and he left the safe door open after ~~every~~ job. [*at least one*]

Summary 3

Streit was caught because someone saw ~~his~~ car; he was sent to prison, and [*an accomplice's*]
he promised to ~~stop~~ breaking the law. In prison, he managed to ~~steal~~ some [*continue* / *make*]
keys and get out. He left all the prison doors ~~open~~. [*locked*]

Summary 4

Streit crossed into Bavaria and tried ~~not~~ to get arrested. This was because
he preferred to be sentenced by ~~an~~ a German ~~Austrian~~ court.

Summary 5

Streit phoned his Austrian warden to say "I'm Sorry." ~~"thank you."~~ He said it was very ~~easy~~
difficult {for prisoners to escape from the Austrian jail.

Summary 6

Streit can~~not~~ be tried by a German court. It is possible ~~certain~~ he will spend a long

time in German prison.

Guessing words from context

You may want to let students work in pairs or groups of three for this
exercise. Answers:
1. collaborators (lines 8–9)
2. deft (line 11)
3. toughest (line 18)
4. caper (line 25)
5. subsequently (line 27)
6. blithely (line 32)
7. cops (line 43)
8. warden (line 52)
9. outstanding (lines 60–61)
10. pondering (line 63)
11. harsher (line 71) or stiff (line 72)

Making connections

After doing the exercise individually, students can compare answers in
small groups. Answers (in these or other words):
1. $330,000
2. stealing money from bank safes
3. a million Austrian schillings
4. Streit, his brother Stefan, and two friends
5. the theft when he left the note and a million schillings behind
6. in the German prison
7. escape from Stein Prison in Austria

Facts and figures

If some of your students are uncomfortable with math, you may want to
have the class work in pairs, with each unmathematical student working
with someone who is good with figures. Let the pairs compare answers
with one another before checking with you. Answers:
1. $11,785.71 ($330,000 ÷ 28 banks)
2. 12.5 (a million schillings ÷ $80,000)
3. 9 months (from March to December)

4. 5 years and 3 months (6 years minus 9 months)
5. 24 (He began in 1970 and was 33 in 1979. 33 − 9 years = 24)
6. in Bavaria's Landshut Prison

ADDITIONAL ACTIVITIES

Discussion

Divide the class into groups of four or five (a group can have only three people in it, but this is not so satisfactory). In this exercise, five points will be discussed. Each student will have responsibility for one or more points, making sure that all the other members of the group express themselves and taking brief notes on the opinions expressed.

   Distribute the points for discussion, either by giving each group an envelope you have prepared, with the five points written on separate slips of paper, or by assigning numbers 1 to 5 to the students and then writing the numbered points on the board. Students will probably work better if you give them a realistic time limit for this exercise. Here are the points:
1. An old and very famous British actress was caught shoplifting (stealing from a store). The story was in all the newspapers. She killed herself before she could go on trial. What do you think of this?
2. What would you do if you found a $5 bill on the sidewalk in front of a grocery store?
3. What do you think of having someone do repairs or cleaning in your home and not declaring it for taxes?
4. What would you do if a cashier in a big department store gave you $10 too much change?
5. What would you do if you saw someone stealing a book?
   You can always let the students run over the time limit if all the discussions are going well; but setting a limit does seem to keep the discussions moving. As the groups discuss, walk around the classroom to give help to students who ask for it. It is better not to correct students' English at this point; you may want to note down for yourself any mistakes that come up often, so you can deal with them in another class. The important thing is that the students communicate with one another in English. If a group finishes early, they can listen to a neighboring group.

Vocabulary work

Ask students to choose five words from the text and determine, by looking them up in the dictionary or asking you, which ones would be proper to use in a statement to a police officer and which are too casual for this. They should then write one or two appropriate sentences with each word.

Writing practice

Give students a choice between two tasks:
1. Write about a theft or robbery you have experienced or read about.
2. Write what you think about different kinds of theft, after the class discussion exercise.

(If students have not done the discussion exercise, you can ask them to discuss one or more of the points from it for writing practice.)

---

15 Great operatic disasters

Warm-up

You may want to introduce the theme of the unit by asking the class to define for you what an opera is and perhaps give you the names of a few famous operas.

Summary skills 1

Once students have done this exercise individually, it would be good to let them compare answers among themselves before checking the answers with the entire class. Answers (in these or other words):
1. soprano / main singer
2. stage / theater
3. mattress
4. jumped / threw herself
5. trampoline
6. bounced / came
7. leave

Summary skills 2

This would be a good exercise for students to do in groups.
   Answers: c, e, h, b, f, d, a, g

Guessing words from context

You might have students compare answers in pairs or small groups before correcting the exercise with the whole class.
   Answers: 1k, 2f, 3j, 4h, 5b, 6i, 7d

Reading carefully for details

Some of the questions in this exercise help students make inferences from what is clearly stated in the text; others make them read details in the text more carefully. When correcting, you will help students if you discuss the "why" of each answer.
   Answers: 1T, 2T, 3F ("It is said . . ."), 4F (". . . is *thought* to be . . ."), 5T, 6F (if they had liked opera, they would have known or learned something about the story), 7F (it was the fault of the producer).

ADDITIONAL ACTIVITIES

Personal disasters

Divide the class into groups of four to six students. Tell students they will have a few minutes to think of a story of some embarrassing experience. The experience can be the student's own or someone else's, and it does not have to be true. Each student should tell the story to the others in the group; the group will vote on the funniest story, which will then be told to the whole class.

Vocabulary work

Ask students to choose four or five words to learn from the text. They should tell another student the reasons for their choices and write two sentences with each word.

Writing practice

Ask students to write down the stories they have told in the *Personal disasters* exercise.

---

16   Poison

Warm-up

Before students open their books, get them thinking about the theme of the text with the following exercise. List these things on the board:
— water from the faucet
— soap
— frozen peas
— shampoo
— fruit juice labeled "100% juice"
Ask the students which of them are likely to contain added chemicals. (Answer: In North America, all of them. Soap and shampoo generally have several chemicals and artificial color. Water from the faucet usually contains chlorine, which is used to purify it. Frozen peas can contain artificial color, and fruit juice is often bought wholesale in concentrated form and then packaged after the addition of chlorinated water.)

Then have the students read the text carefully, stopping as often as they like. Remind them that it is not important to understand every single word if they get the general meaning.

Summary skills

After students have worked on the exercise individually, let them compare answers in small groups before checking with you. The missing descriptions (in these or other words):

3. Dioxin sold to Bliss.
4. Dioxin sprayed on roads, riding arenas (1971).
5. Birds and horses killed, people sick.
7. Piatt went to EPA and State Division of Health (1972).
9. Much later, dioxin found with rabbit test (1974).
12. Many people still sick (now).

Guessing words from context

When you are correcting this exercise, find out what mistakes were made and discuss why they were made. This will help students the next time they need to guess unknown words.

Answers: 1d, 2g, 3k, 4a, 5e, 6l, 7b, 8h, 9m

Making connections

Let students compare their answers in small groups after doing this exercise individually. Answers:
1. the rabbits
2. the federal government
3. the St. Louis suburb of Times Beach
4. Northeast Pharmaceutical and Chemical Co.
5. Bliss' trucks
6. Piatt

Reading carefully for details

This exercise requires students to read carefully for specific points. The "doesn't say" feature of this exercise is designed to make students read more carefully and avoid making unwarranted inferences.

Answers: 1F, 2F, 3DS, 4F, 5T, 6T

ADDITIONAL ACTIVITIES

Compensation and prevention

Divide the class into groups of five or so. Give them two minutes for each group to elect a chairperson (who must see that the tasks are done and that everyone in the group is consulted) and a secretary (who must take notes on the results of the discussion). Then give the groups the following tasks to perform:
1. Make a list of people or organizations who made mistakes leading to "the poisoning of Missouri." Decide what each did (or did not do) to be considered guilty in this affair.
2. One billion dollars ($1,000,000,000) has been awarded to the dioxin victims in Missouri by the courts. Decide what percentage of this money should be paid by each person or group in question 1.
3. Make at least four recommendations to the legislature of the State of Missouri for new laws to ensure that this sort of situation cannot happen again.

Make sure that everyone understands the tasks before they begin. Then walk around the room to answer questions while the students are working. Try not to intrude on a group unless your help is requested, and do not correct the students' English mistakes at this time. You can do more controlled language work at another time; in this discussion students should be developing their fluency and their ability to make themselves understood in English.

Students will probably enjoy sharing the results of their work with the other groups when the exercise is finished.

Vocabulary work

Ask each student to choose five words from the text to learn – words that could be used in a story that had nothing to do with chemicals. They should look the words up in the dictionary and write one or two sentences with each.

Writing practice

Encourage students to refer back to the text for help with language as they do one of these exercises:
1. Write about a disaster that has happened (or about an imaginary one) in your own country or a place you know.
2. Write a short science fiction story, and include a disaster.

Part 5 Persuasion: Why you should do it

17 The family room

Warm-up

Before students open their books, introduce them to the theme of the text in the following way: Tell them to imagine that they manufacture well-built, comfortable, traditional furniture and that they want to advertise it. Get them to give you all the ideas they can think of on how to advertise it and what points to stress.

   Then have them read the text, taking their time and stopping if they wish. Tell them that the advertisement is by the type of furniture company they have been thinking about.

Summary skills

Let students do the exercise individually and then compare answers in small groups before checking with you.
   Answers: 1d, 2f, 3c, 4a, 5g

Guessing words from context

Students can do this exercise in groups of two to four so they can share their ideas. Answers:
1. theater
2. bad
3. problems of society
4. bad
5. crowded / with too much work to do

Inference

This exercise requires some thinking. Let students work on question 1 individually and then compare their answers with the students around them before checking with you. Answers: a and c, Yes; b and d, No

   Then let them think about the second question for a few minutes and explain their viewpoint to other students. You may want to ask for volunteers to give their views to the class.

ADDITIONAL ACTIVITIES

Class survey

In this exercise, each student is assigned one of the questions given here. Ask each student to interview as many of the other class members as possible in 15 minutes, and then give a brief report to the class. Fifteen questions are given here. If there are more than 15 people in your class, you can give the same question to more than one person and tell them to compare their answers before giving a joint report. If you have a very small class, you may want to give each person more than one question. Omit any questions that are not relevant to your students.

1. Do you think advertising is: good / bad / both good and bad?
2. Cigarette smoking has been shown to cause lung cancer. Should cigarette ads be banned or controlled in some way? Explain.
3. What do you think of ads that use women in swimsuits to sell things like cars?
4. How influenced do you think you are by advertising: not at all / a little / a fair amount / a lot?
5. How influenced do you think most people are by advertising: not at all / a little / a fair amount / a lot?
6. Do you think you respond better to an ad that uses humor or one that "gives facts"?
7. Try to quote three advertising slogans right now.
8. Do you usually read ads in magazines or do you skip them?
9. Would you / do you enjoy working for an advertising agency?
10. What do you think of television commercials directed at small children (for toys, candy, etc.)?
11. Do you watch the commercials when you watch television? Why / Why not?
12. Have you ever bought a product because it was offering a contest with a big prize?
13. Do you feel that you have sometimes learned things from advertising that you really wanted to know?
14. Have you ever bought anything from a mail-order catalogue? If so, were you satisfied with it?
15. Some magazines have as many pages of advertising as pages of articles. This means the reader does not pay the real cost of the magazine. Would you rather pay more and have fewer ads?

Vocabulary work

Have each student choose four unfamiliar words from the advertisement, look them up in the dictionary, and write one or two sentences with each.

Writing practice

Ask each student to write an advertisement. It can be serious or funny, and can be for a product, an event, or a cause. It should be at least 100 words long.

18   Better left unsaid

Warm-up

Ask students to vote by a show of hands on whether it is all right to tell the following lies:
— telling someone on the phone that a person is not at home, when the person just doesn't want to speak on the phone
— telling your boss/teacher that you are late in the morning because of bad traffic, when actually you overslept
— telling someone you like his or her shirt when you actually don't
Then tell the students that the text is not about lying, but about not telling the whole truth. Have them read it, taking their time and stopping when they want.

Do you have the main ideas?

This exercise is likely to provoke a certain amount of discussion, so you may want students to do it in groups of three or four. Walk around the classroom while they are working to give any help that they need.
      Answer: The four main points are 1, 3, 4, and 5.

Guessing words from context

Let students do the exercise individually. Then correct it with them, examining any wrong answers and helping them see why they are wrong.
      Answers: 1d, 2m, 3k, 4e, 5a, 6h, 7j, 8b

ADDITIONAL ACTIVITIES

Discussion

Divide the class into groups of four or five (a group can have only three people in it, but this is not so satisfactory). In this exercise, four points will be discussed. Each student will have responsibility for one or more points, making sure that all the other members of the group express themselves on that point, and taking brief notes on the opinions expressed.
      Distribute the points for discussion, either by giving each group an envelope you have prepared, with the four points written on separate slips of paper, or by assigning numbers 1 to 4 to the students and then writing the numbered points on the board. Students will probably work better if you give them a realistic time limit for this exercise. Here are the points:
1. A married person is in love with someone else, but is not going to do anything about it and does not want to leave the marriage. Under what circumstances should the other partner be told, if at all?
2. A grandmother has given her grandchild a very precious gift, something that has been in the family for years. The grandchild has lost it. Under what circumstances should the grandmother be told, if at all?

3. One of three teenage children is adopted. The parents have never talked about this, but one of the children has learned the truth. Under what circumstances should that child tell the adopted child, if at all?
4. A person is applying for a very responsible job involving decisions that can put people's lives in danger. Several years ago, this person was treated by a psychiatrist for depression, but this problem has never come back and the person feels completely cured. Under what circumstances should the person tell the people who are offering the job, if at all?

You can always let the students run over the time limit if all the discussions are going well; but setting a time limit does seem to keep the discussions moving. As the groups talk, walk around the classroom to give help to students who ask for it. It is better not to do any correction of the students' English at this point; you may want to note down for yourself any mistakes that come up frequently, so you can deal with them at another time. The important thing is that the students communicate with one another in English.

If a group finishes early, they can listen to a neighboring group.

Vocabulary work

Ask students to each choose five adjectives from the text that they would not normally use in their own writing, check the meanings in the dictionary, and write one or two sentences using each one.

Writing practice

Ask students to give their own opinions about "telling it like it is," or to choose one of the topics from the class discussion to write about.

19 Save the children

Warm-up

To introduce the theme of this unit, you might ask if someone in the class knows what a charity is, or tell the class if no one knows. Ask them if they know the names of any charities and what they do.

Summary skills

This exercise gives students the opportunity to choose for themselves which aspect of the text they wish to focus on. Have students do the exercise individually first; then ask each student to find at least one other person who has chosen the same topic. They should compare notes and write a set of notes they both agree on. Answers will vary somewhat, but students' final notes should look something like this:

1. SCHOOL
   - it is miles away
   - Maria would like to go to school
   - Maria can't go because she's needed at home
   - sponsorship will buy school supplies
   - a combined sponsorship can build a school

2. MARIA'S MOTHER
   - has lost her husband and two children because the family couldn't afford a doctor
   - needs Maria's help at home
   - could farm her land if given tools and guidance
   - could earn money if given help

3. FOOD AND WATER
   - not enough food for Maria's family
   - the water available to Maria's family is contaminated
   - food could be grown on Maria's mother's land if tools and guidance were given
   - clean water could be brought to Maria's family if enough sponsorship were received

4. SPONSORING A CHILD
   - costs only 52 pennies a day
   - could help Maria's mother farm her land and earn money
   - combined with other sponsors' money, yours can help people help themselves through schools, health facilities, clean water
   - rewards through correspondence, photos, progress reports, knowledge that you're really helping

5. MARIA'S FAMILY LIFE
   - her father, a brother, and a sister have died
   - she takes care of her baby brother
   - she helps her mother with the chores

Guessing words from context

In correcting this exercise, find out what mistakes students have made and help them see why their answers are wrong. This will help them do better the next time.

Answers: 1c, 2f, 3d, 4j, 5l, 6a, 7g, 8i

Why and how?

This exercise gives students practice in inference. You may wish to have them do it in small groups. Answers:

1. contaminated water
   not enough food
   fatigue from too much heavy work
2. Maria's father died because the family could not afford a doctor.
3. tools for her mother
   guidance for her mother
   a school in the village
4. clean water
   a health facility
   growing her own food
5. photographs
   progress reports
   letters

ADDITIONAL ACTIVITIES

Planning help

This is a group exercise in which the students imagine they are in charge of planning help for Maria's village.

Divide the students into groups of five or so and give them the following task description. Make sure that they all understand what they have to do. While they are working, move around the classroom to give any help they may need. Do not correct any mistakes they may make in their English; this exercise is for developing fluency, and they can work on the correctness of the English at another time. When the groups have finished (you may want to impose a time limit before they start), ask each group to state and briefly explain its results.

Task: You are the committee in charge of planning aid to Maria's village. Sponsors have been found for all the children; this means that you can help the individual children, but also that you can begin work on larger projects. The problem is that your money from the sponsors arrives only once a month. Here is a list of projects you wish to carry out, and the number of months of money each project will take. You must decide the order in which the projects will be done. Be prepared to tell the rest of the class why you have decided on this order.

1. Tools and seeds for farming – one month
2. Sewing machines so the women can earn money – three months
3. Clean water facilities – six months
4. School building – five months (the government will provide a teacher)
5. Health facility – ten months
6. A radio antenna so the village can get educational programs and news – two months
7. More land so the village can sell produce in the nearby town – nine months
8. A tractor to help work the new land – five months

Vocabulary work

Ask students to choose four unfamiliar words or expressions from the advertisement, look them up in a good dictionary, and write two sentences using each word.

Writing practice

Have each student write a letter of appeal like the one here, on behalf of a favorite charity. The charity can be real or imaginary.

---

20   Two letters

Warm-up

Note that in the United States most people have to pay their doctors for care given; often people have private insurance policies, which reimburse part of their medical expenses.

You may want to get students thinking about the theme of the unit like this: Tell them to imagine that they do not have enough money to pay all their debts. They must make a choice between paying
– their monthly installment on the car,
– their doctor's bill, or
– their life insurance.
Get students to vote with a show of hands on which bill they would pay.

Do you have the main ideas?

This exercise covers the main points in the two letters.
Answers: 1F, 2T, 3F, 4T, 5F

Guessing words from context

This exercise is slightly more challenging than some of the other *Guessing words from context* exercises; you may want students to do the exercise in pairs or groups in order to pool their resources. Answers:
1. account
2. extend the courtesy of replying
3. ignore
4. ample
5. alternative
6. collection agency

Inference

Students can do this exercise in pairs, since the "cultural" content of the letters may be new to some students. Answers:
1. Ms. Marques is the "Office Manager"; this would imply that there are other people working in the office.

2. In the first letter, Ms. Marques invites the man to make "partial payments . . . even small payments."

3. Ms. Marques leaves the man several options in both letters: "even small payments"; "send payment, call, or write." In her last paragraph she does not threaten to turn the account over to a collection agency if he does not pay, but rather to do so if she has not heard from him.

4. If the account is turned over to a collection agency, the fact will be "on [the man's] credit record." This implies some centralization of credit information.

ADDITIONAL ACTIVITIES

Role play

This exercise takes a little preparation. You will have to copy the role descriptions below: Description A for half of the students, and Descriptions 1B, 2B, and 3B in roughly equal numbers for the other half. The students will work in pairs (A + 1B, A + 2B, A + 3B); but if there is an uneven number in the class, you can give out an extra 1B role and let two students play spouses going to the office together.

Hand out the roles, giving the same role to students seated in the same part of the classroom. Tell them to read the role description and discuss it with one another; answer any questions they have about meaning. Then pair the students up, an A and a B in each pair. Remind them before they begin their conversations that some of them will be standing when the conversation begins and some of them sitting. They can consult their own role description during the conversation but should *not* look at the other person's.

Walk round the classroom while they are doing the exercise, to give help to those who need it. It is a good idea not to interrupt the students during this exercise to correct their English mistakes; let them practice speaking freely with the English they can command. Students who finish early can form new pairs.

Role descriptions

A: You work in Dr. Brown's office. If patients come in to talk about a bill, you ask them to sit down, and you consult their file. You are very understanding if the people seem to be in financial difficulty. However, you must try to get them to begin paying something immediately, if only $1 a week. Experience has proved that the sooner people begin paying, the more likely they are to pay the entire debt. Once the patients agree on payment arrangements, ask them to try not to miss a payment.
Here are some extracts from your files:
Mr. (or Ms.) Edmundson owes $200
Mr. and Mrs. Honeywell owe $350
Mr. and Mrs. Thompson owe $300
Ms. Wells owes $50
Mr. (or Ms.) Wood owes $150

1B: You are Mr. or Mrs. Honeywell. You owe Dr. Brown $350 for Mrs. Honeywell's treatment. Mr. Honeywell has been on strike for a month. Mrs. Honeywell doesn't work outside the home and has two children under five at home. Mr. Honeywell has been trying to find temporary work but has not been successful. You do not want your debt to be referred to a collection agency. You can begin paying $50 a month when the strike is over. Begin the conversation by saying. "Hello, I'm Mrs. (Mr.) Honeywell. I'd like to talk to you about my bill."

2B: You are Mr. or Ms. Edmundson. You owe Dr. Brown $200. You are a single parent with a child of six. The child's school fees have just gone up; on top of that, your car has broken down and you have had to buy another one. You cannot possibly pay the $200 now; you would like to pay $20 now and $20 a month until the summer (in three months' time). Then you may be able to pay a little more. Begin the conversation by saying, "Good morning (afternoon). I'm Mr. (Ms.) Edmundson. I'd like to discuss my bill."

3B: You are Ms. or Mr. Wood. You owe Dr. Brown $150. You are a university student and have very little money. You cannot borrow money from your parents because you have quarreled with them. Your part-time job gives you just enough money to live on, and you do not want to take on any more paid work now, because your studies may suffer. You would like to wait until the summer (three months from now), when you will have a full-time job. You can then pay off the $150 within two months' time. If the people in the doctor's office are really insistent, you may be able to pay $10 a month until the summer.

Writing practice

1. Have students imagine they are the patient's father or mother and write a reply to the March 17 letter, apologizing for not writing sooner and proposing some arrangement for payment.
2. Have students write another letter from Ms. Marques to the patient's father, dated March 30. He has not answered any of the letters and his account is to be turned over to a collection agency.

21   Men and women: Some differences

Warm-up

Before students open their books, get them thinking about the theme of the unit by asking whether they think men's or women's bodies are stronger. Get them to vote by a show of hands and then ask a few students to explain their votes.

Then have them read the excerpt, taking as long as they want and stopping as often as they like. Remind them that they do not need to understand every single word, but need only get the general meaning.

Summary skills

Let students work in groups of three or four to complete the table. Then get the class to help you put the completed table on the board. It might read like this:

	Men	*Women*
Blood manufacture	Less efficient (line 1)	More efficient (line 1)
Breathing	Deeper, less often; more polluted air (lines 2–6)	Not so deep, more often; less polluted air (lines 2–6)
Lead in bodies	More in boys (lines 10–15)	Less in girls (lines 10–15)
Bones	Larger (line 16)	Smaller (line 16)
Shoulders	Broader (line 19)	Narrower (line 19)
Pelvis	Narrower (line 19)	Broader (lines 20–21)
Climbing	Easier (lines 25–26)	More difficult (lines 26–29)
Skin	Thicker, not so soft; doesn't wrinkle easily (lines 30–33)	Thinner, softer; wrinkles easily (lines 30–33)
Fat – amount?	Less (lines 40–41)	More (lines 34–35)
Fat – where?	Doesn't say	In layer under skin (line 34)
Percentage of muscle	41% (lines 41–42)	35% (lines 42–43)
Strength – percentage of weight	90% (lines 44–45)	50% (lines 45–46)
Energy reserves	Fewer (lines 51–52)	More (lines 51–54)
Capacity for exercise with aging	Goes down greatly (lines 55–61)	Goes down only a little (lines 55–61)

Guessing words from context

You can use the correction of this exercise as a learning activity by examining with the class any wrong answers, and helping them see why those answers are wrong.

Answers: 1j, 2d, 3l, 4a, 5g, 6i, 7e, 8b, 9m

Inference

This exercise calls both on students' understanding of the text and on their knowledge of the world, which they must apply to the information in the text. Let them work individually for a few minutes, and then have them compare their answers in small groups before checking with you. Answers:
1. People bleed during surgery; since men do not manufacture blood as efficiently as women, they cannot replace the lost blood as fast.
2. The brain, since lead in the body lowers intelligence.
3. Women's, since their thighs are joined to their knees in such a way as to make climbing difficult; this must certainly put an extra strain on the knee.
4. The man would wrinkle less, and the woman would stay cooler.
5. The man would still be stronger. 90% of his weight is strength at age 20; $20 \times (60\%$ of that strength at age 60$) = 54\%$ of the same weight. For a woman, 50% of her weight is strength at age 20; $20 \times (90\%$ of that strength at age 60$) = 45\%$ of the same weight.

ADDITIONAL ACTIVITIES

Finding jobs

Divide the class into groups of four or five. Each group should find four jobs that women would do better than men, based on the information in the article, and four jobs that men would do better than women. They should note down the reasons for their choices. A representative from each group should then visit all of the other groups in turn and explain his or her group's choices.

Vocabulary work

Have students find five words in the article that do not have to do with the human body and that they think will be useful to them in their own writing. They should look the words up in the dictionary and write one or two sentences using each one.

Writing practice

Ask students to write briefly what they think the psychological and/or intellectual differences between men and women are.

22   Getting to the airport

Warm-up

If there are several students in the class who have flown before, find out how many of them feel relaxed in an airport and how many of them worry about missing their plane. If there are no students who have flown, ask students whether they think they would be more worried about missing a plane than about missing a train or long-distance bus.

Then have them read the column, taking their time and stopping if they want. Remind them that it is not essential to understand every word, as long as they get the general meaning.

Summary skills

Have students work in pairs or threes to complete the table. Completed table:

	Early-airport person	Result	Late-airport person	Result
Worries?	Yes	Ulcers, heart attacks, etc.	No	No bad results
Luggage on plane?	First	Last off plane	Last	First off plane
Anxious about seat?	Yes	Never gets seat he or she wants	No	Always gets a seat
Marriage partner?	Late-airport person	Arguments	Early-airport person	Arguments

Guessing words from context

This would be a good exercise to do in pairs or small groups. Answers:
1. stroll (line 4)
2. justice (lines 6, 10)
3. round (line 18)
4. conspiracy (line 62)
5. stumbled (line 84)
6. guts (line 87)

Inference

In this exercise, students must infer from the descriptions of early-airport people and late-airport people how they would act in situations not discussed in the text. Let students work individually and then compare their answers in small groups before checking with you. Answers:
1. The early-airport person would begin studying immediately, three weeks before the test; the late-airport person would begin studying the night before.
2. Early-airport people pay their telephone bills when they receive them;

late-airport people pay their telephone bills when the phone company threatens to cut their line off.

3. The possibilities here are numerous: pack several days ahead of time, buy travel insurance, stop the newspapers from being delivered, ask a neighbor to water the plants and collect the mail, etc.
4. An early-airport person's luggage is often searched by customs officers, even though there is never anything illegal in it, because the person looks so nervous. A late-airport person's luggage is never searched.

ADDITIONAL ACTIVITIES

Class survey

In this exercise, each student must do a survey of the rest of the class, walking around and asking everyone else a question. When the survey is finished, each student makes a brief report to the class. Fifteen questions are given here. If there are more than 15 people in your class, you can give the same question to more than one person and tell them to compare answers before giving a joint report. If your class is very small, you may want to give two or more questions to each student.

1. Have you ever flown in an airplane? If so, how old were you when you flew for the first time?
2. Have you ever taken a charter flight? Would you take one (again)? Why?
3. Would you like to fly in a Concorde? Why?
4. Would you enjoy being an airline pilot for a year? Why?
5. What would you rather do – pilot a plane or pilot a glider (which is like a plane but has no engine)?
6. Do you think a flight attendant's job is exciting? Why?
7. Would you rather travel by train or plane? Why?
8. Do you / would you feel safer in a plane or in a car on a fast road? Why?
9. What are the advantages of air travel?
10. What are the disadvantages of air travel?
11. Can you name a famous male airplane pilot? a famous female airplane pilot?
12. Would you feel as comfortable flying with a male airplane pilot as with a female one?
13. Would you rather have a male or female flight attendant serving you in a plane, or doesn't it matter?
14. If you could have a free airplane ticket to anywhere in the world, where would you go?
15. If it became possible in your lifetime for you to take a rocket to the moon, would you like to do it? Why?

Vocabulary work

Ask students to find three new words in the text, or three words they know used in new ways. They should look these words up in a dictionary and write one or two sentences using each word.

Writing practice

Ask students to write about a trip they took that involved some kind of problem.

---

23   How personality affects your health

Warm-up

Before students open their books, you might want to introduce the theme of the unit by putting the six questions from the beginning of the text on the board. Explain the meaning of *hard driving* and *excel* if you think your students need these, but don't explain any other words.

Put the students into pairs. Each student should try to guess how his or her partner would answer the six questions, and then check with the partner to find out the real answers.

Reading for specific information

Explain that the students have an exercise to do before they read the text. Working individually, they should try to answer the seven questions as quickly as they can. You may want to explain that this is a kind of reading that they are likely to have to do in their future studies or work. Answers:
1. eight years (line 10)
2. nearly two thousand (lines 10–11)
3. get his or her hair cut (lines 18–19)
4. no (line 24)
5. women with children, who were married to blue-collar workers and were holding down clerical jobs at the same time (lines 34–36)
6. yes (lines 38–39)
7. no (lines 45–46)

Inference

Let students read the article as carefully as they want, stopping as often as they like. Then have students do this exercise individually, comparing answers in small groups before checking with you.

Answer: All the statements except 2, 6, and 8 are likely to be true of Type B people.

Guessing words from context

Put the students into groups of three or four to do this exercise. Ask them to try and agree on all the answers. Walk around while they are working to give any help that is needed; if there are difficulties, you may want to point out some of the contextual clues that can be used. Answers:

1. pressed for time (line 4)   5. achiever (line 39)
2. The chances are (line 13)   6. stiff (line 41)
3. hassle (line 29)   7. grasp (line 44)
4. keep on top (line 32)

Making connections

Some of the items in this exercise are very challenging. For example, in
number 1, not all the students may be aware that *them* is used in an
informal style as a pronoun for singular items like *someone* and *everybody*.
In order to avoid students' getting discouraged, you may want to do this
exercise as a class, asking volunteers to give the answers and giving further
explanations where there seem to be difficulties. Answers:
1. someone who is being long-winded
2. working women
3. some housewives (the ones who felt the same time pressures as women
    with outside jobs)
4. *Those:* The housewives
    this: that things would get out of control unless they tried all the time to
    keep on top
5. some of those you work with
6. the conflict

ADDITIONAL ACTIVITIES

Brainstorming: Therapy for Type A people

This activity is best done in small groups of about five people. Each group
has three tasks:
1. The brainstorming itself. During this time the members of the group
    must try to think of as many ways as possible for Type A people to
    become more like Type B people – and consequently become less likely
    to have heart attacks. One group member should act as secretary and
    write all the ideas down. Any idea, no matter how nonsensical it seems,
    should be expressed: It is quantity, not quality, that matters at this
    stage. A seemingly ridiculous idea can sometimes spur a creative and
    practical one. You should probably give a time limit to this part of the
    exercise.
2. Feasibility rating. The group should give each idea a feasibility rating
    from 1 for an easy-to-carry-out, inexpensive project to 4 for an almost
    impossible idea.
3. Effectiveness rating. The group should take the five or so most feasible
    ideas and rate them according to how far they will go toward helping
    the Type A people: **A** for a very effective idea, **B** for an effective idea,
    and so on.
You may want the groups to report their findings to the class when they
have finished, but this is a case where the process is more important than
the product, and the reporting can easily be dropped.

Vocabulary work

Ask each student to choose five words or expressions from the text to learn, and tell another student why he or she has chosen these words. Then have students look up their words in the dictionary and write one or two sentences using each one.

Writing practice

Ask students to imagine that they have a close friend who is a Type A person and who has just had a heart attack. They should write a letter to the friend, suggesting how changes in his or her life-style might reduce the chances of another heart attack. They should try to use some of the words and expressions from the text in their letters.

---

24   Wonder wander

Warm-up

To introduce this unit, ask students to name all the things that can be found on a typical street in your town. Spend a few minutes listing these on the board.

Summary skills

This will help students define the broad divisions in the poem.
   Answers: 1, 9, 14, 19, 24

Guessing words from context

You may want to ask students to compare answers before correcting this exercise with the whole class. Answers:
1. leather; documents / letters / papers / work
2. stop
3. bird / fowl ("chicken" is also a plausible answer given what the students know)
4. bird

Vocabulary links

This is a good exercise for group work. Answers:
1. take walks, stroll, shoes, stride, parade, wander, soft-shoed, easy-legged, sidewalk
2. talk, voices, whisper

3. ducks, geese, bird-trees, puppy dogs, lady bugs, turkey hens, sea gull
4. clothes, hats, dresses, shoes, pockets, soft-shoed
5. eyeing, wild eyed, glances, watching, see, look

Attitudes and feelings 1

This exercise is designed to stimulate discussion in the classroom. There are really no "right" answers. The answer to the first question might be "business men" or "young men"; the answer to the second question might be "children" or "the narrator." You can handle the exercise in several ways; here are two examples:

1. Get a show-of-hands vote on the first question. Have each student find another student who has given the same answer and discuss the reasons for two minutes; then have all the students change partners. This time they might be with someone who has a different point of view. They get two more minutes to exchange views and return to their seats. Handle the second question in the same way.
2. An open-class discussion. One way to make sure students listen to one another is to have them observe the following rule: No one can give an opinion until he or she has restated the opinion of the last person to speak, to the satisfaction of that person.

Attitudes and feelings 2

This is an exercise that can profitably be done in a group; it will probably provoke some discussion. Answers:

children (e)	young men (f)
business men (h)	me (b)
young girls (a)	

ADDITIONAL ACTIVITIES

Vocabulary work

Ask students to choose four or five words to learn from the text. They should look the words up in a good dictionary and find out, perhaps from you, if the words could be used
— in a business letter
— in a conversation with a six-year-old.
They should try to use the words in the next exercise if they are appropriate, or to write a sentence or two using each word if not.

Writing practice

This poem is about people walking in a town. Ask students to write a poem or story about walking in a different place, for example, the forest, the mountains, the country, a big city. They can describe different people walking in different ways if they want.